INSTANT
TURNAROUND!

INSTANT
TURNAROUND!

GETTING PEOPLE EXCITED

ABOUT COMING TO WORK

AND WORKING HARD

HARRY PAUL AND **ROSS RECK, Ph.D.**

wm

WILLIAM MORROW
An Imprint of HarperCollins*Publishers*

INSTANT TURNAROUND! Copyright © 2009 by Harry Paul and Ross Reck. All rights reserved. Printed in the United States of America. No part of this book may be used or reproduced in any manner whatsoever without written permission except in the case of brief quotations embodied in critical articles and reviews. For information address HarperCollins Publishers, 10 East 53rd Street, New York, NY 10022.

HarperCollins books may be purchased for educational, business, or sales promotional use. For information please write: Special Markets Department, HarperCollins Publishers, 10 East 53rd Street, New York, NY 10022.

FIRST EDITION

Library of Congress Cataloging-in-Publication Data has been applied for.

ISBN 978-0-06-173042-9

09 10 11 12 13 OV/RRD 10 9 8 7 6 5 4 3 2 1

To all the management gurus for the
knowledge they have shared with us
and the differences they have made

CONTENTS

INTRODUCTION

Do you have a company, department, team, or sales force where the employees routinely under-achieve, fail to take initiative, refuse to work together as a team, or intentionally sabotage the success of your organization? Would you like to turn your situation around immediately—as in overnight? Think something like this is impossible? Think again!

Early in 2007, Tom Coughlin, head coach of the New York Giants of the National Football League, was in danger of losing his job. His team had lost seven of their last nine games and was character-ized by in-fighting and bickering. Coach Coughlin had always been a no-nonsense, hard-nosed football coach who motivated his players with fear. During the off-season he completely reversed his approach to coaching and started motivating his players with trust. He started smiling, let his players get to know him as a person, and communicated to his players in a number of ways that he cared about them. The turnaround was instant. The team came together and the players gave Coach Coughlin everything they had, week in and week out, which culminated in a 2008 Super Bowl victory over the previously unbeaten New England Patriots.

If you'd like to create the same kind of turnaround, continue reading this book. You'll find that achieving an instant turnaround is something anyone can do. What's more, you won't have to wait a month, six weeks, or a year to see results; you'll notice significant improvement the very first day! The method is easy to implement, costs nothing, and everybody wins.

INSTANT
TURNAROUND!

CHAPTER 1
A SERIOUS PROBLEM

*New York, New York—An informal gathering of
prominent management gurus. Attendees include:
Dr. Thomas "Tom" Schweppes, a university
professor from the U.K. and author of* How to
Recognize and Reward Employee Performance.
*Tom is an affable senior citizen with a zest for
life and a heart as big as the outdoors. "Electron
Joe" Scott, author of* Winning with People, *which
details his experiences as a legendary CEO. Joe is
an outspoken messenger about what's wrong with
corporate America and what needs to be done to
fix it. Dr. Maxwell "Max" Maxum, author of* The

Magic of Being Nice. *Max is a devoted family man who is committed to spreading the word about principle-centered living. Freddie Kim, author of* The Authentic Manager. *Freddie is a self-effacing and friendly person and the junior member of the group. His passion is converting his observations and ideas into effective management practices that produce immediate results. . . .*

The group was chatting as Freddie entered the room accompanied by a woman none of them had met.

"Freddie, you brought a guest," said Max.

"This is my mom, Nancy. With me living in San Diego, we haven't spent much time together lately, so we thought it would be fun to spend a weekend in New York. She's the executive vice president of Biz Trenz, *the highly successful magazine that targets fast-growing and progressive companies. I'm sure you're all familiar with it," he said proudly.*

"Wow! Yes, we are, and we're glad you came," said Tom.

"Thanks," she smiled.

"You've been holding out on us, Freddie. You never told us your mom was a business executive," said Max.

"Sorry about that. It just never occurred to me to tell you."

Tom changed the subject. "I really look forward to these times when we can get together to catch up on what we're working on and share our stories about what works when it comes to motivating employees. We don't do it nearly enough."

"I agree," said Joe. "You know, the last time we did this was almost two years ago."

"I guess we need to do something about that," said Max, the informal convener of the group. "So, who'd like to start us off?"

"I would," said Tom. "I had a plant manager contact me a little over a year ago after he had been to one of my programs. He was panicked because the productivity in his plant had fallen off and he was in danger of not meeting his quarterly profit goal. He'd had several meetings

3

with his employees to let them know that their performance was not acceptable, but they were not responding. So he asked if I had any suggestions on how to turn this around."

"What did you tell him?" asked Freddie.

"I told him to circulate through his plant several times a day and act like he cared about his employees. I asked him to call me in two weeks and let me know what happened."

"What did he say?" asked Joe.

"He thought I was joking at first, but when he found out I was serious, he agreed to give it a try."

"Did he call you?"

"He did and he was totally blown away by how quickly things had turned around and how he was back on track toward meeting his goal."

"That's a great story," said Max. "I have a sales example I'd like to share. A vice president of sales for a large pharmaceutical company was very concerned about his sales numbers. After being flat for months, his numbers were starting to slide. Trying to turn things around, he required each member of his sales force to make two extra sales calls a day, but this wasn't getting the job done. He asked me what I thought he should do next."

"What did you tell him?" asked Joe.

"To cut the number of calls that each salesperson had to make each day in half, and instead of focusing on making sales calls, to have his staff focus on building long-term relationships with their customers."

"What did he say to that?"

"He was stunned at my suggestion, but after we talked about how customers prefer to buy from salespeople they like and trust, he reluctantly agreed to try it."

"Did you find out what happened?" asked Freddie.

"I did. He called me a year later and was he ecstatic! His sales had increased by 95 percent over the previous year. He told me he was thinking about cutting the number of calls that his salespeople had to make each day even further. His comment was, 'Focusing on building long-

term relationships is far more productive than focusing on sales calls.'"

Max leaned back in his chair and said, "You know, none of this is rocket science. We've known since the 1920s that paying positive attention to the people who work for you has a dominant impact on their productivity. That's the message all of us believe in and focus on in one form or another. And each of us has dozens of examples that show how the payoff for doing this is incredible, and the impact is immediate. Yet we're still not seeing wholesale, across-the-board implementation. We're still seeing and hearing from a lot of unhappy workers out there. Why do you think this is?"

"That's a good question," said Freddie. "I think there's a disconnect between our people message and the executives and managers we're trying to reach."

"What do you mean?"

"Almost every executive and manager I talk to is quick to admit that people are their most

important asset, but they don't live *it—they pay lip service to it, but don't take action. In reality, they behave as though the opposite is true."*

"I agree," said Tom. "Most tell me that their biggest challenge is that they have so many unhappy employees. They know what this is costing them in terms of low productivity and high turnover. When I tell them they could turn their situation around tomorrow by treating their employees with respect and giving them the positive attention they want, they look at me like I'm nuts."

Joe chimed in, "I had a CEO come up to me after a seminar and ask if this people stuff really worked as well as I claimed. I said, 'Absolutely, that's how I ran my company.' He asked if I could give him another example of where it worked successfully and I gave that to him. Then he asked for another and so on. Finally, after the fifth example, he looked at me, scratched his head, and then turned and walked away. I don't think I could have convinced him if I had a thousand examples, and I told him so."

7

EXECUTIVES AND MANAGERS
CAN BE VERY SLOW LEARNERS

Between 1924 and 1932, a series of experiments were conducted at a Western Electric plant in an attempt to find out what affected employee productivity. They found that the simple act of paying positive attention to employees had the dominant impact on their productivity. Today, nearly a century later, we're still finding that the vast majority of employees are unhappy in their jobs because their management doesn't care about them or notice what they do. This leads to low productivity and high turnover. At the same time, executives and managers, almost across the board, are saying that low productivity and high turnover are their biggest problems. Hello! What's there not to get? Start treating your employees with respect and giving them the positive attention they want and these problems will turn around **instantly**!

"What did he say?" asked Max.

"That there's got to be more to it than that."

"I had a similar incident happen to me," said Freddie. "A manager came up to me during a break at one of my programs and said, 'What you're saying makes absolute perfect sense, and I can't poke holes in any of your arguments, but it's so counter to what I've been told over the years that I just can't buy it.'"

"This is a serious problem," said Max. "Many of the very people we're trying to reach don't want to hear our message. Why is that?"

"I'll tell you why," said Joe. "It's because most managers, especially those in senior positions, aren't all that concerned about people because they're so preoccupied with performance numbers and the bottom line."

"He's right," said Tom. "They fully understand that the harder their people work, the better those performance numbers are going to be. What they refuse to accept is that the better *they* treat them, the harder they'll work."

"So, how do we turn this around?" Max asked.

The room then went silent as everyone thought. After about a minute, a feminine voice spoke up and said, "We had a situation at Biz Trenz some years ago similar to the ones you've been describing. I don't want to sound like I'm bragging, but I was instrumental in turning that situation completely around. Would you like to hear my story?"

At this point the silence in the room was deafening as everyone was focused on Freddie's mother, eagerly waiting to hear what she was going to say next. . . .

NUGGETS FROM CHAPTER 1

One lesson many executives and managers don't get:

1. They are very concerned about performance numbers and the bottom line.

2. Most fully understand that the harder employees work, the better those numbers are going to be.

3. <u>What many don't get is that the better they treat their employees, the harder they'll work.</u>

CHAPTER 2
A SHOW OF COURAGE

"For those who don't know, Biz Trenz is located in Chicago, about ten minutes from Midway Airport. Besides the magazine, the company produces motivational products such as posters, calendars, books, and CDs that it markets through its catalogs, website, and ads in Biz Trenz. At the time, Biz Trenz was not a pleasant place to be. Many of the employees hated coming to work, so they routinely underachieved. Turnover was high as was absenteeism, and teamwork didn't exist. I was the director of human resources and occasionally wrote articles for the magazine.

Our CEO, Josh Tabor, or J.T., as he preferred to be called, managed the place with an iron hand. Every morning my stomach tightened up as I pulled into the parking lot.

"On this particular day, J.T. had called a meeting of senior managers in his office to unveil his new management system. Attending the meeting were: Tom Russell, the editor; Bill Robertson, the director of advertising; Trent Foster, the director of production; and myself. I had just replaced the previous human resources director who was fired for openly disagreeing with J.T. . . ."

. . . . .

It's no secret that things aren't going well around here," said J.T. "Our performance numbers, across the board, are terrible. I'm convinced it's because we aren't getting enough effort out of our employees. So, I've decided to tighten things up by implementing a new management system that

I call **Management by the Numbers**. I've spent a lot of time developing this system and I think it's just what the doctor ordered to turn this company around. Let me tell you how it works: First, we make it very clear to the managers and employees what performance numbers they're expected to achieve. Second, we strike the fear of God into them by informing them of the consequences that will occur if they don't. Third, we go to our offices and continually monitor their actual performance numbers on our computers to make sure they compare favorably to expectations. Fourth, if they don't, we get out there and kick some butt. So, what do you think?"

"I think you're spot on, J.T.," said Bill. "This new system of yours will give *Biz Trenz* the shot in the arm it needs."

"I don't see how it can miss," said Tom. "Sheer genius."

Trent chimed in, "If I had to describe this new system of yours with a single phrase, it would be 'bulletproof.'"

J.T. smiled as he liked what he was hearing. "And what do you think, Nancy?"

"I hate to be the one to say this, J.T., because I know you spent a lot of time and effort figuring out this new system. Also, keep in mind that when I say what I'm about to tell you that I have the best interests of you and *Biz Trenz* at heart. But, I can't see how this new system can improve our situation. In fact, it will probably make matters worse."

J.T.'s jaw dropped. He was not used to being challenged by his subordinate managers—let alone by the only woman in the group. The three other senior managers stared at Nancy in disbelief, apprehensive about how J.T. might respond.

"What do you mean, it won't work?" he said, trying not to lose his composure as his face began to turn red.

"Your new system is trying to motivate our employees by scaring them so they'll work harder. These people aren't slaves, they're employees. Many of them have one foot out the door already because they hate working here. If you implement this new

16

system, it's only going to make their decision to leave that much easier. Pretty soon, the only people who'll be working here are those who can't get jobs anywhere else. If you think productivity is bad now, just watch how bad it gets after all our good employees have left."

J.T. winced as he listened to Nancy's last comment.

Nancy continued, "What we need at *Biz Trenz* is a management system that gives our current employees a reason to stay and a reason to apply their best efforts toward performing their jobs."

"And I suppose you have such a system in your human resources bag of tricks?" J.T. said sarcastically.

"No, I don't, but if you give me a week, I bet I can find one."

Much to everyone's surprise, J.T. said, "You're on, but don't even think of coming back with one of those touchy-feely gimmicks like the ones we've tried in the past. If you remember, each time we tried one of those things there would be a short

17

spurt of increased productivity and then, when the novelty wore off, productivity fell back to where it was, which wasn't good. Instead, I want you to come back with a management system that works—one that will instantly send the productivity of this company through the roof and keep it there. Have I made myself clear?"

"That you have, J.T.," she said as she stood up to leave, "that you have. . . ."

. . . . .

"That took a lot of courage to stand up to your CEO like that," said Joe. "I'm impressed."

"In hindsight, I suppose you're right. I remember walking out of J.T.'s office feeling a bit weak in the knees, thinking, What have I gotten myself into? I had been widowed for a little more than a year, my mother was in a nursing home, and I was raising my high school–aged nephew while my younger sister was going through drug

18

rehab. So, I really couldn't afford to suffer the same fate as my predecessor. On the other hand, it felt like the right thing to do, and besides, I had a plan—sort of."

"What do you mean?" asked Freddie.

"When I was in college, before I met your father, I dated a guy named Jack Sims."

"Do you mean the guy who took over struggling ValuFirst Airlines and turned it into a moneymaker overnight?" asked Max.

"That's him."

"He's a living legend among CEOs. His airline has turned a profit for twenty straight years," said Tom.

"His story is amazing and his office is at Midway Airport. So, the next morning I called ValuFirst and asked to be put through to him. . . ."

. . . . .

"**H**ello, **Jack.** This is Nancy Kim."

"Nancy, it's great to hear from you. It's been a long time. Say, I'm really sorry to hear that your husband passed away."

"Thank you, Jack. It's been over a year, but I still miss him. Fred was the best."

"What can I do for you?"

"I've been following your success at ValuFirst and I'd like to pick your brain to learn about any management secrets that are behind your success."

Jack laughed as he said, "Let me be the first to tell you that there are no secrets, but I'd be happy to share with you what I know."

"When do you suggest we start?"

"Do you have any free days next week?"

"Right now, they're all pretty free."

"Then why don't you come to Midway Airport at eight-thirty Monday morning and we'll go on a field trip."

"What kind of field trip?"

"We'll take a quick flight to St. Louis and back. I

want you to see ValuFirst in action before I explain how we do things."

"How will I find you?"

"I'll meet you at the ValuFirst ticket counter."

"Thank you so much, Jack. I want you to know I really appreciate this."

"I'm looking forward to it. See you on Monday. . . ."

NUGGETS FROM CHAPTER 2

Managing employees strictly by the numbers sends all these wrong messages:

1. Performance numbers and the bottom line are more important than employees.

2. Managers don't trust their employees.

3. Employees are expendable.

4. Managers don't care about the well-being of their employees.

These messages not only motivate employees to be far less productive, they also provide a strong incentive for the better performing employees to seek employment elsewhere.

CHAPTER 3

AN EYE-OPENING
FIELD TRIP

"When I arrived at the ticket counter, there was Jack, smiling and joking with some of the ticket agents. After we spent some time catching up on each other's lives, I proceeded to tell him about the challenge I was facing at Biz Trenz. . . .*"*

. . . . .

"So you work for J.Tv.," he said.

"Do you know him?"

"I sure do. We go way back. In fact, we were in the Army together."

"Really."

"Yes. He and I still see each other occasionally. He's a really fun guy in a social setting, but I don't think I'd like working for him. He and I are on the opposite ends of the spectrum when it comes to motivating employees. I'll bet working at *Biz Trenz* is anything but fun."

"That's for sure, and that's why I'm here—to see if I can figure out a way to turn our situation around."

"Well then, let's get started. I suggest we get our boarding passes first and then find a place where we can do some observing," he said as he handed Nancy her round-trip ticket for their St. Louis flight.

The line in the ticketing area was quite long, but it moved quickly. When it was their turn to check in, a middle-aged man recognized Jack and waved them over to his counter. "Jack!" he exclaimed as he reached out to shake Jack's hand. "It's great to see you."

"It's great to see you, too, Bill. How are things going?"

"Couldn't be better. Where are you going?"

"We're taking a quick trip to St. Louis and back," he said as they handed Bill their tickets and driver's licenses.

"Business or pleasure?" he asked as he examined their tickets.

"A field trip," said Jack as he winked at Bill.

"Sounds like fun." Then Bill looked at Nancy and said, "You're in for a memorable day. Jack conducts great field trips."

"Now for the fun part," said Jack as he guided her to a spot where they could observe the entire ValuFirst ticketing area. "Let's just watch for a while and see what goes on."

After twenty minutes, Jack turned to Nancy and said, "Has anything impressed you so far?"

"I'll say! I now understand why that line of passengers moves along so quickly—these ValuFirst employees are really working hard. Just look at all the multitasking that's going on. They're printing boarding passes and attaching luggage tags *while* they're talking to the passengers or to each other."

"Have you noticed anything about their attitudes?"

"You bet! They're all smiling. This tells me they enjoy being here and like what they're doing. I also noticed all the ValuFirst employees are wearing buttons that have the letters TGIM printed on them. What does that stand for?"

"Thank God It's Monday," replied Jack, smiling.

"Amazing," said Nancy, shaking her head.

"Did you notice any supervisor or manager out there cracking the whip?"

"That's the thing that really struck me. If there is a boss in the area, I would be hard pressed to tell you who it is."

Jack looked around for a few seconds and then said, "It's the blond woman with the khaki slacks and the white shirt. You can tell because she has a walkie-talkie attached to her belt along with a set of keys. Let's watch her for a few moments and see what she does."

As they watched, this woman moved up and down the row of counters looking for opportunities to keep the operation running smoothly. She took baggage tags from agents and attached them to bags. At one point she carried an elderly woman's bags over to security. As she did all this, she continually interacted with the passengers. A man in a wheelchair was particularly amused with what she had to say. When an agent asked for her assistance with a problem, she immediately jumped behind the counter and helped him or her solve it.

"She's actually working harder than the agents and she seems to really enjoy what she's doing," said Nancy.

"Have you noticed how the agents respond to her when she shows up at their counter?"

"They seem genuinely happy to see her," said Nancy.

"Why do you suppose that is?"

"I'm not sure."

"It's because they know she's not coming to look over their shoulder or point out mistakes. She's there to lighten their load."

WHICH KIND OF LEADER ARE YOU?

Recently we received an e-mail containing the following quote: "There are two types of leaders: those interested in the flock and those interested in the fleece." Effective leaders are those interested in the flock—the people they're leading. They see their role as that of a *giver*—to get behind their people and support them in ways that bring out their best. Ineffective leaders are interested only in the fleece and couldn't care less about their flock— they're *takers*. Takers usually don't last very long or get very far because the people they're trying to exploit don't care about them and therefore don't give them their best efforts. Givers, on the other hand, last longer and go farther because they have a loyal flock that is looking out for them and is willing to go through walls for them if necessary. The lesson here is to be a giver and show an interest in your flock. If you do, your flock will respond in ways that will guarantee your success as a leader.

"As I continue to watch her, it seems like her full-time job is making people's days."

"It is," replied Jack with a twinkle in his eye. "Now, let's go through security and see what's going on at the gate area."

As they arrived, a plane was pulling up to one of the gates. "Come with me over by the window," said Jack. "I want you to see something." As they walked, he asked Nancy, "How long do you think it will take the employees of ValuFirst to turn this plane around?"

"I really have no idea, but if I had to guess, I'd say forty to forty-five minutes—but that's only a guess."

"I want you to note the time when the plane comes to a stop at the Jetway and let's see how much time elapses before the plane pushes back. I also want you to watch what happens out there."

As soon as the plane came to a complete stop, people and equipment seemed to appear out of nowhere. On the side of the plane opposite the Jetway, provisioning trucks pulled up to the front and rear doors to replenish the galley and remove the trash. Motorized conveyor belts pulled up to the front and rear cargo doors to facilitate the off-loading of baggage, mail, and freight. At the same time, a refueling truck parked under the wing and the driver began refueling the plane. It was like watching a tightly choreographed dance routine. Each person knew his or her job and they performed it efficiently and quickly.

When provisioning was completed, the drivers parked their trucks and jumped into the cargo bays to help with the off-loading. As soon as the baggage, mail, and freight were off-loaded, the crew began loading the baggage, mail, and freight for the next flight. When the plane was loaded, the cargo doors were closed and it was ready to be pushed back. Just then, a small pickup truck pulled up alongside the rear cargo door. The driver opened the cargo door and threw in two pieces of last-minute baggage. As soon as the cargo door was closed, the plane started moving back out onto the tarmac.

"How long did it take?"

"Seventeen minutes! That was truly awesome. It was like a beehive out there. And to think that an entire planeload of passengers came off the plane and another planeload of passengers boarded, with all their carry-on baggage, during those seventeen minutes. All I can say is wow."

"It's even more amazing once you realize that this same scenario gets repeated several thousand times a day at airports all across the country—365 days a year. The majority of ValuFirst's flights are turned around in twenty-five minutes or less."

"I'm beginning to see why it's such a profitable airline," said Nancy.

Fifteen minutes before flight time, the gate agent began the boarding process. As they walked down the Jetway, Nancy said, "I'm impressed by how much your employees seem to love what they are doing. The work environment at ValuFirst seems to bring out the best in people."

"It does," said Jack.

As the plane taxied toward the runway, the flight attendant in the front began to give what turned out to be a very entertaining safety briefing. At one point, he said, "While there may be fifty ways to leave your lover, there are only six ways to leave this aircraft: two forward exit doors, two exits over the wings, and two aft exit doors." Later in the briefing he said, "We will be flying over the Mississippi River and hundreds of swimming pools this afternoon on our way to St. Louis, so in the event of a water landing, your seat cushion can be used as a flotation device." He concluded with, "Pushing your reading light button will turn on your reading light, but pushing your flight attendant call button will *not* turn on your flight attendant."

"That guy was really having fun as he gave the safety briefing," Nancy laughed.

"That's right. Having fun goes hand in hand with being excited about what you're doing."

When the plane reached its cruising altitude, the flight attendants moved efficiently through the cabin passing out snacks and taking drink orders. Once all the passengers were served, the flight attendants worked their way up and down the aisle, visiting with the passengers. One of the flight attendants learned that it was a passenger's birthday, so she led the plane in singing "Happy Birthday."

"Don't they ever give it a rest?" asked Nancy. "It's like their switches are always in the 'on' position."

"When you're excited about what you're doing, you have no desire to put your switch in the 'off' position—you'd miss too much fun."

The rest of the short flight to St. Louis was pleasant and uneventful.

Their return flight was scheduled to leave at 3:20 and, as expected, it left on time. After they had been served their beverages and snacks, Nancy looked over at Jack and asked, "What is it about working here that gets people so excited about what they're doing? Let's face it, most of these jobs at ValuFirst—issuing boarding passes, loading baggage, serving snacks, and cleaning planes—are boring, repetitive, and mundane. Yet the employees perform them with pride and enthusiasm."

"I'd rather not try to answer your question now in this confined space with nothing to write on. Since tomorrow's my day off, why don't we get together at my home office around eight-thirty," he said as he handed her a card with his address and cell phone number on it.

"Sounds great. See you then. . . ."

· · · · ·

"That was some field trip you went on," said Joe.

"It certainly opened my eyes to what's possible when it comes to motivating employees. I've never seen people working harder and enjoying it more. The whole scene was remarkable—the minute I walked into the ValuFirst ticketing area I could feel the energy and excitement radiating from the employees. I couldn't wait to find out what the management of ValuFirst was doing that was behind all this."

NUGGETS FROM CHAPTER 3

Happy employees:

1. Smile more.

2. Have more fun.

3. Work harder.

4. Work better with fellow employees.

5. Love their boss.

Bottom Line: Happy employees are *productive* employees.

CHAPTER 4
DESTINATION: WORK

"The next morning I arrived at Jack's home with my notepad in hand. After what I'd observed the day before, I was ready to listen and learn. . . ."

. . . . .

As they entered Jack's office, Nancy asked, "How does ValuFirst do it?"

"Do what?" he asked smiling.

"Get its employees excited about working hard doing repetitive mundane tasks day in and day out?"

Jack thought for a few seconds. "If our success could be attributed to any one thing it's this: Every manager, supervisor, and team leader at ValuFirst understands how to tap into the *discretionary effort* of our employees."

"What do you mean by discretionary effort?"

"People regulate the amount of effort they put into their jobs based on how they feel they're being treated by their boss. If they feel they're being treated well, they will become excited about giving their absolute best efforts, which means they'll work way beyond their job descriptions. If they feel their efforts are unappreciated, they'll pull back and do only what they have to do to keep their jobs. And if they feel they're being abused, they'll either get even by figuring out a way to sabotage their boss's performance numbers, or they'll look for a job somewhere else."

"The job of a manager then is to treat people in such a way that they become excited about applying all their discretionary effort toward their jobs."

"That's right—that's what drives performance numbers and the bottom line."

"And how do you go about doing that?"

"When my management team and I took over at ValuFirst, the place was a mess. We had the worst customer service in the industry, morale was low, employee turnover was high, and the company was on the verge of going bankrupt. All we did was transform our workplace from a place that people dreaded coming to into a place that people looked forward to coming every day—and the rest is history."

"How long did it take before you saw changes in productivity and morale?" asked Nancy.

"The turnaround was instant. Once our employees saw that my management team and I were on their side, things changed in a hurry. We noticed big time improvement the first week we took over."

"Why was the turnaround so immediate?"

"Because turning work into a destination is all about people, and people respond very quickly to positive treatment. For example, if someone pays you a complement, how long does it take before you feel good? Do you have to wait a week, a month, or a year?"

"No, you feel good right away."

"It's the same thing when you start treating people right at work. They start to feel good about where they are and what they're doing right away, and they respond accordingly by working harder."

Jack continued, "Let me share with you the program we developed to make that happen here at ValuFirst. It's called *Destination: Work*," he said as he picked up a marker and wrote the two words on his whiteboard:

Destination: Work

"As I said, our goal at ValuFirst is to make work a destination—a place that our employees get excited about coming to every day. We want it to be a place where they feel appreciated and cared for—a fun place where people come to get their batteries recharged. We want it to be the kind of place where our employees wake up in the morning and say, 'Wow! I get to go to work today—lucky me!' instead of saying, 'Poor me. I guess I have to go to work today.'"

"That explains all the TGIM buttons I saw yesterday."

"That's right."

"So what exactly needs to be done in order to turn work into a destination?"

"Let me share with you the first step of our program," he said as he turned to his whiteboard and wrote:

> • Focus on People as Well as Performance Numbers

"Trying to manage by focusing only on performance numbers is like trying to coach a football team by focusing only on the scoreboard. The problem with doing so is that the scoreboard isn't going to score any points for you; it only keeps track of them. It's the people on the field who score the points, so that's where your attention needs to be focused."

"You're not saying that managers should focus solely on their people and ignore the performance numbers, are you?"

"Not at all. If you watch any successful football coach, you'll notice that he regularly glances at the scoreboard to stay apprised of the current game situation, but he doesn't stare at it the whole game through. The overwhelming majority of his attention is focused on getting the best efforts out of his players—the people who do the work necessary to score the points."

"What does focusing on people involve?" asked Nancy.

"As a manager, you have to understand that

people come to work motivated to satisfy **their** needs, not yours. Once you understand this, all you have to do is meet those needs and your employees will put forth the necessary effort to take care of the performance numbers and bottom line."

"It sounds so simple."

"It is, and boy does it work. In fact, it's the only thing that does work. You saw it in action yesterday."

"If focusing on people and meeting their needs works so well, why doesn't everyone manage this way?"

"That's an excellent question. It's because managers at most other companies are preoccupied with performance numbers and the bottom line. So they focus on those numbers—trying to meet their own needs—and they completely ignore the needs of the people who do the work to make those numbers happen. Instead, they try to *force* them to perform at a certain level either by looking over their shoulders and micromanaging them, or by threatening them with negative consequences if they don't."

PUTTING EMPLOYEES FIRST—THE KILLER MANAGER PHILOSOPHY

Why do Toyota, Southwest Airlines, Costco, and Starbuck's lead their respective industries in terms of profitability? Answer: They operate from a management philosophy that says employees come first and customers come second. As former Southwest CEO Herb Kelleher put it, "Your employees come first. If they're treated right, they'll treat your customers right, and if your customers are treated right, they come back, and that's good for stockholders." But hold on, there's more. Research studies show that companies who put their employees first also reap the following additional benefits: Their employees:

Work harder
Perform a higher quality of work
Take more initiative
Are more accountable
Are not afraid of change
Work better with fellow employees

As you can see there is no downside to putting employees first, just a very bright and profitable upside.

"Let me illustrate the difference." Jack then looked at Nancy and said, "Here's what I would like you to do. In the family room next door, you'll find three lazy, old cats sleeping on the couch. I want you to go in there, wake them up, and herd them into the kitchen at the other end of the house."

"I've heard more than one person say that herding cats is impossible because they're so independent."

"Have you ever tried to do it yourself?"

"No, I haven't."

"Then how do you know that it can't be done?"

"I guess I don't really know for sure."

"Then I want you to give it your best try. Who knows, you just might prove that old cat cliché wrong."

Nancy went into the family room and woke the cats up one at a time. As she woke each of them, they stood up, stretched, yawned, and blinked their eyes. She then tried to herd them into the kitchen by making a shooing motion with her arms. When she did this, one cat immediately jumped off the couch and made a beeline for the living room across

45

NO ONE LIKES TO BE MICROMANAGED

No one likes to be micromanaged—even the people doing the micromanaging. As children, we hated it when our parents looked over our shoulders, and as adults we resent it when our bosses do it. Bosses who micromanage do so in an attempt to control the performance of their employees. The theory is: The more tightly you control them, the harder they'll work. In reality, the opposite is true, because micromanaging tells your employees that you don't trust them. Without a climate of mutual trust, no employee is going to give you their best efforts—they'll only give you what they have to in order to keep their jobs. So, if you want your employees to get excited about working hard on your behalf, back off and support them. Show them that you have faith in their abilities and let them know that you're on their side. Then, get out of their way and allow them to make you look good as their boss.

the hall. The second cat leaped to the floor and ran behind the couch. The third cat hissed at her and looked determined to hold her ground.

"Are you making any progress?" asked Jack, smiling as he walked into the room.

"Well, I've proved to myself that herding cats is impossible."

"Given that cats can't be herded, if you truly wanted those cats in the kitchen right now, how would you go about getting them there?"

"The only thing I can think of is to pick them up one at a time and carry them into the kitchen."

"There is a much easier and quicker way to get the job done."

"What's that?"

"Focus on *their* needs instead of yours."

"I'm not sure what you mean."

Then Jack handed Nancy a can of cat treats and said, "Take this into the kitchen and shake it so that it makes a loud enough noise that the cats can hear it at this end of the house."

Nancy took the can and headed toward the

47

kitchen. When she arrived, she began to shake it vigorously. Within seconds, all three cats came running into the kitchen, meowing demandingly and began circling her feet.

"Notice anything different?" asked Jack as he entered the kitchen.

"I'll say. Shaking this can of treats brought these cats into the kitchen in a hurry!"

"Yes, it did, and I think it would be a good idea if you gave each of them the treats they're expecting now."

"You mean I'd better follow through and take care of their needs?"

"If you want them to get excited about running into the kitchen again, you had better," he said with a smile. "Now, let's take a look at the two methods that you used to try to get these cats into the kitchen. With the first method, herding, you tried to *force* the cats into the kitchen. When you tried that, you were focusing on *your* needs—getting the cats into the kitchen—and not those of the cats. You could have expended lots and lots of effort and still not succeeded in getting them into the kitchen. With the second method, shaking the can of treats, you focused on the *cats'* needs. In doing so, you got those same stubborn, independent cats to do *exactly* what you wanted. Now let me ask this: What was the attitude of the cats when you tried to herd them?"

"They were definitely not happy, nor were they willing to cooperate. In fact, one was quite resentful about me trying to herd her."

"What was their attitude when you shook the can of treats?"

"They were happy, they were excited, and they came running."

"That's right. They applied all their discretionary effort toward doing exactly what you wanted and they *loved* you while they were doing it.

"The same thing holds true for people. When you try to force people to perform, whose needs are you focusing on?"

"Yours."

"And what are you using as a motivator?"

Nancy thought for a moment and then said, "If you're using force, the motivator has to be *fear*."

"And does fear bring out the best in people?"

"No, it brings out their worst."

"Now let me ask you this," said Jack. "If you expect to get employees excited about applying all their discretionary effort toward performing mundane repetitive tasks day in and day out, whose needs do you have to focus on?"

"Theirs."

"Exactly. And when you focus on their needs, what are you using as a motivator?"

"I hate to admit it, but I have no idea."

"This brings us to the second step of our *Destination: Work* program," he said as he wrote on his board:

- Motivate with Trust Instead of Fear

Nancy studied what Jack had just written for a few seconds and said, "I've never thought of *trust* as a motivator before."

"Most people don't consider trust a motivator, but trust is absolutely necessary if you expect to tap into the discretionary effort of your employees. You saw yesterday how hard the employees at ValuFirst work and how much they enjoyed it. Do you think they would do that for a manager they didn't trust— someone who didn't care about them and was only out to use them?"

"No, they wouldn't."

"When people trust their manager, they know that he or she is going to take care of them—they know that if they work hard, their manager is going to reciprocate in some meaningful way. As a result, it's in their best interest to apply all their discretionary effort toward performing their jobs."

"Is developing trust with the people who work for you a difficult thing to do?"

"That's the beauty of it. It's really easy. All you have to do is circulate among your employees and execute four simple behaviors. I refer to them as *The Four Be's*." Jack then turned to his board and wrote:

THE FOUR BE'S FOR MOTIVATING WITH TRUST

- **Be Real**
- **Be Appreciative**
- **Be Interested**
- **Be Nice**

Nancy carefully studied the four bullet points for a few seconds and said, "It's all about the basics, isn't it?"

"It has to be, because the basics are the only things that work when it comes to motivating people to work hard. . . ."

. . . . .

"At this point Jack was out of coffee, so he suggested we walk back to the kitchen and refill our cups. I was thankful for the break as both my arm and wrist were tired from taking so many notes."

"This guy is a real fountain of knowledge," said Max.

"He sure is and he practices what he preaches."

NUGGETS FROM CHAPTER 4

The goal of *Destination: Work* is to create a work environment where employees:

1. Are excited about coming to every day.

2. Feel appreciated and cared for.

3. Come to get their batteries recharged.

4. Wake up in the morning and say: "Wow! I get to go to work today. Lucky me!"

CHAPTER 5
THE FOUR BE'S

"When we returned to the office, Jack immediately walked over to his whiteboard. . . ."

. . . . .

"Let's talk about ***being real***. What do you suppose that means?"

"Being yourself and letting the real you shine through."

"That's right. It means that you don't try to come across as someone who is superior to those around you. When you motivate with trust, there is no room for arrogance. Instead, you have to reach out and embrace those around you—you have to become one of them."

"That's like the boss we observed at the ValuFirst ticket counter yesterday. She didn't walk around arrogantly barking out orders and pointing out mistakes. She worked right alongside the people she was supervising, and they were glad to see her when she showed up. In fact, she blended in so well she was actually hard to spot."

"That's an excellent illustration of the point I was trying to make."

"Can we move on to *being appreciative*?"

"You bet," said Jack. "People absolutely love to work hard when their efforts are appreciated."

"I'm going to play devil's advocate for a minute," said Nancy. "Why is that?"

"Because being appreciated is one of the strongest needs people have—they crave appreciation almost as much as they crave food. So, if you as an executive, manager, supervisor, or team leader make it a point to regularly thank your employees for the

"REAL PEOPLE" CAN ACHIEVE AMAZING RESULTS

When he was CEO of the Chrysler Group, Dieter Zetsche was credited with turning a "stumbling Detroit automaker" completely around. Shortly after he accepted the position to go back to Germany and head up all of DaimlerChrysler, *USA Today* listed some of the things he did that contributed to his success: ". . . he had such a 'regular guy' image that he was simply known by his first name to most people." The article went on to say that "he won approval at Chrysler by jumping in instead of standing aloof. He answered all of his e-mail personally. He ate in the regular cafeteria with the lower-ranking employees. He attended a union conference shortly after he took over and stayed until he fielded all the questions from wary United Auto Workers members." The moral to the Dieter Zetsche story is this: When you are a "regular person"—open, honest, approachable, humble, and respectful—people will respect you, work hard for you, and will see to it that you are incredibly successful. What's there not to get?

things they have done on your behalf, they'll give you all or most of their discretionary effort."

"This is consistent with one of the things that keeps showing up in employee surveys. Most employees say they would be more than willing to put more effort into their jobs if their bosses would just come around and say thank you once in a while. But since their bosses don't, their attitude is, 'why bother?'"

"There you go. Nothing is more demotivating than going the extra mile and having your boss not notice or care."

"I'm impressed at how tightly all this fits together," said Nancy. "Can we talk about **being interested**, what's that all about?"

"It's about treating people like they really are your most important resource. After all, it's their level of effort that determines your performance numbers and the bottom line."

"And how would you go about doing that?"

"By getting out of your office and getting

A LESSON FOR MANAGERS: YOU CAN'T SAY "THANK YOU" TOO OFTEN

A research study recently reported in the *Harvard Business Review* found that the vast majority of employees are quite excited when they start a new job. This study also found that in 85 percent of the companies surveyed, this excitement declines sharply after the first six months, and continues to decline for years afterward. One of the big reasons is that their managers didn't take the time to thank them for a job well done, yet these same managers were quick to criticize them for their mistakes. What these managers fail to realize is that if they would focus their efforts on showing sincere appreciation to their employees instead of pointing out mistakes, their employees would work harder and make far fewer mistakes. Saying "thank you" often not only energizes your employees, it makes you a more effective manager.

involved with your employees—get to know them, let them get to know you, ask their opinion on things and listen to what they have to say. And make sure you give them your undivided attention when you're listening."

"This goes back to focusing on people and meeting their needs. Talking is all about meeting your needs while listening is about meeting theirs."

"That's right. It's hard for most of us to fathom, but those around us really don't want to hear us talk about ourselves. At the same time, they're dying to tell their story to someone who cares. Effective managers understand this and this is one of the things that sets them apart from everyone else. They realize that telling their story to their employees will not improve the performance of their team, department, plant, or company one bit. But listening to *their* stories will—it shows that you care, which strengthens the level of trust."

"This is all so simple."

"It is," replied Jack. "And as you saw yesterday,

MANAGING BY WANDERING AROUND SENDS THE RIGHT MESSAGES

Managing by Wandering Around, or MBWA, is the practice of putting a smile on your face and casually circulating among your employees for the sole purpose of visiting with them. Emphasis during these informal visits is on showing an interest in your employees and listening to what they have to say. Doing this on a regular basis greatly enhances your effectiveness as a manager because it sends the kind of messages that your employees are dying to hear: First, the fact that you're even doing this tells them that you're accessible, approachable, and that you think they're important. Second, your willingness to listen to what they have to say tells them you care. This is the kind of boss everyone wants to work for and the kind of work environment where employees get excited about giving their best. If you aren't already doing this, try it for a week and watch what happens. You'll be amazed at the results.

it works extremely well. Now let's take a look at the fourth and final bullet. What do you suppose *being nice* is all about?"

"Being pleasant to be around—the kind of person everyone is happy to see come to work."

"And the most important part of being nice is your smile."

"Why is that?" asked Nancy.

"Your smile draws people toward you. It tells people that you're open, approachable, and that you care—the kind of person they want to get to know better."

Jack continued, "The other aspect of being nice is saying or doing something that brightens the day of each person you come into contact with—greeting them by name, complimenting them on something they've done or what they're wearing."

"I'm going to play devil's advocate again, because I want to make sure I understand this. Why is being nice so important?"

"Being nice is what makes people like you. You

see, people have to like you *before* they'll trust you, and they have to trust you before you can tap into their discretionary effort."

"I have to say that making the The Four Be's part of your daily routine sounds like fun."

"Is it ever, and that brings us to the third step of our *Destination: Work* program," Jack said as he once again wrote on his board:

> ● Turn Work into Fun

"Now that we've created an atmosphere of trust, we're all free to be ourselves and turn our work into fun—just like the flight attendant who gave the entertaining safety briefing yesterday. So why not take advantage of the opportunity? Turning work into fun makes even the most mundane and routine tasks enjoyable."

"So this is why the employees we observed at ValuFirst all had smiles while they worked hard and

BEING NICE IS A KEY INGREDIENT TO YOUR SUCCESS AS A MANAGER

How many times have you heard people say something like, "If you're nice, people will take advantage of you"? Or, "If you're nice, people will think you're a pushover"? Or, "Nice people finish last"? People who say these things are totally out of touch with reality and haven't bothered to check out the facts. A study reported in the *Harvard Business Review* found that being likable—making those around you feel good about themselves—is more important to your success than how competent you are. A similar study reported in the *Wall Street Journal* found that being a nice approachable person who listens, goes hand in hand with being a highly successful manager. Peter Handal, CEO of Dale Carnegie Training in New York, put it this way: "It's not enough to just be good at what you do. In my experience, the people who reach the top are nice."

why their switches were always in the 'on' position—
they were having fun."

"That's right. And when you're having fun, what
you're doing never gets old or boring, which means
you look forward to coming to work every day—
especially on Monday."

Nancy looked away, thought for a few seconds,
and then turned to Jack and said, "I think I got what
I came for. Spending these past two days with you
has been an eye-opening experience. My only problem now is how do I get a person like J.T. to embrace
a program like this?"

"That's going to be a challenge, all right. I
wish you all the luck in the world. And if you
think I can be of any help, feel free to call me
anytime. . . ."

. . . . .

*"I knew J.T. wouldn't sit still or keep quiet long
enough to allow me to explain* Destination: Work
to him verbally. So I spent the next three days

writing a detailed report on how it worked. I remember thinking as I finished it: J.T. is going to come unglued when he reads this."

"Destination: Work *is the exact opposite of J.T.'s* Management by the Numbers *program. Weren't you concerned about getting his buy-in?" asked Freddie.*

"You bet I was, but I also knew that J.T. couldn't turn down a challenge."

<u>NUGGETS FROM CHAPTER 5</u>

Managing with trust frees employees up to turn their work into fun. As a result:

1. The most mundane and repetitive tasks become enjoyable.

2. Employees look forward to coming to work every day—especially on Monday.

3. Employees apply more of their discretionary effort toward performing their jobs.

CHAPTER 6
THE CLASH

"I arrived at work early on Monday morning. Before going to my office, I placed a copy of my report on J.T.'s desk. I knew he wasn't going to like it, and I remember thinking to myself, this is going to be an interesting day. I was in the middle of dealing with the horde of e-mails that had accumulated during my absence when J.T. stormed into my office with my report in his hand. His face was red and he was upset. . . ."

. . . . .

"**W**here did you come up with this touchy-feely garbage?" he screamed.

Nancy looked him in the eye and said firmly, "Look, you asked me to find a management system that works, and there it is. You call it touchy-feely, but the truth is that managing is all about tapping into the discretionary effort of our employees."

"Discretionary effort!" he shouted. "What's that, the latest touchy-feely buzz phrase?

"And what's with the idea of making work a destination—a place where employees can turn their work into fun? I'm running a business, not a country club."

"Look, I know this stuff works—I've seen it with my own eyes at ValuFirst Airlines."

"Oh, it sounds like you've been talking to Jack Sims."

"That's right."

"Look, Jack is a great guy and a good friend, but when it comes to running a company, he's the high priest of touchy-feely."

"What do you have against treating employees with respect and paying positive attention to them?"

"Let's just say it's not my style."

"So, are you saying that his style hasn't made ValuFirst a success?"

"We're not talking about ValuFirst, we're talking about *Biz Trenz*."

"J.T., I have so much confidence in *Destination: Work*, that I'm willing to make a bet with you. You let me work with your worst performing department here at *Biz Trenz*, and if I can't turn it *completely* around in ninety days using this program, you can fire me."

A smile came over J.T.'s face, because he loved nothing better than winning a bet. "I'll do you one better. I have a certain department in mind and if you can turn that department around in ninety days, I'll promote you and I'll publish the report you just gave me as a cover story in *Biz Trenz*. But, between you and me, I don't think you have a prayer of succeeding," he said condescendingly. "That department is in really sorry shape."

"You're on, J.T.," she said defiantly. "Which department is it?"

"It's the Direct Mail and Order Fulfillment Department. Their Quality/Productivity Index, or QPI as we like to refer to it, is a three—the lowest in the company. I don't know what's wrong over there. Mike Sutton, the manager, seems to be tough enough on his people, but he isn't getting results. If you can work with Mike and get the department's QPI up to a nine or above, I will concede that you've turned the department around."

"But that's a 300 percent improvement!"

"You're the one who just said, 'let me work with your worst department.' You're not going to chicken out now, are you?"

"No, I'm not."

J.T. called Mike. "Hello, Mike? This is J.T. Say, I'm sending Nancy Kim over to your office. I want her to work with you over the next ninety days to

THE HIGH COST OF POORLY TRAINED SUPERVISORS

In their book *The Invisible Employee*, Adrian Gostick and Chester Elton estimate the cost of employee turnover in America to be 1.7 trillion dollars annually. That's a huge drain on American businesses. They also cite studies which point out that the biggest single reason people quit their jobs is the behavior of their immediate supervisor— they were either abusive, didn't care about them, didn't listen, didn't notice or appreciate what they did, or were only out for themselves. Believe it or not, there's good news in all of this. If American businesses would simply teach their frontline supervisors how to interact more effectively with the people who work for them, they could reclaim the lion's share of those 1.7 trillion dollars. We're talking about basic behaviors like being nice instead of nasty or indifferent, noticing the things employees do and saying thank you. These behaviors don't sound all that profound, but if the majority of frontline supervisors in America effectively executed these behaviors, it would fatten the bottom lines of American businesses by more than a trillion dollars—now that *is* profound.

help you shape up your department and get your QPI up where it belongs. Whatever she asks you to do, I want you to do it, no matter how strange it may sound. And believe me, some of her ideas are going to sound pretty strange. Can I count on you for that? Good. She'll be there shortly."

Then J.T. smiled as he turned to her and said, "It might interest you to know that the people who work for Mike refer to him as 'Iron Mike' Sutton. I think you just might have bitten off more than you can chew."

"We'll see," she said with a determined look as she headed for Mike's office.

As Nancy approached Mike's office, she saw him standing in the doorway with his arms folded across his chest scowling at her. *This is going to be a memorable experience*, she thought.

"So, you're here to show me how to do my job."

Nancy looked at Mike and smiled. "No, I'm here to win a bet with J.T."

"What do you mean?"

"I spent part of last week at ValuFirst Airlines

learning about a method of managing that is so superior to the way we manage people here at *Biz Trenz*. It's called *Destination: Work*."

"What did J.T. think of this method?"

"He referred to it as touchy-feely garbage."

"J.T. thinks anything short of using a club is touchy-feely garbage."

"Exactly, that's why I made the bet with J.T."

"Tell me about this bet."

"I told J.T. that if he would let me work with his worst-performing department using *Destination: Work*, I would turn it completely around in ninety days. If I didn't then he could fire me."

"I guess it's no secret that I have the worst-performing department in the company. So, how did J.T. respond?"

"He said that if I did turn it around, he'd promote me and run my report as a cover story in *Biz Trenz*. He thinks I don't have any chance of succeeding."

Mike's arms finally came down from his chest and a smile came over his face. "What I hear you

THE TRUE MEANING OF TOUCHY-FEELY

   "Touchy-feely" is a condescending term used to put down management tools that openly focus on people and meeting their needs. The connotation is that such tools are somehow grossly inferior to the more common hard-nosed management tools that use fear as a motivator and ignore people's needs. What touchy-feely really means is that people have *feelings* and they need to be personally *touched* in ways that make them feel good if you expect to bring out their best. On the other hand, there isn't a hard-nosed management tool on the planet that will bring out the best in people—they all bring out people's worst.

saying is that if you pull this off, J.T. is going to have to eat some crow."

"That's right."

"Boy, that would really be something to see. I must say, you've piqued my interest."

"Before you get too excited, there's one catch."

"What's that?"

"In order to win the bet, we have to get your QPI score up to a nine."

"Wow! That's an incredibly tall order. I must say that I admire your courage. Where do we get started?"

"Let's take a tour of your department so we can get a feel for where things are."

"Okay, let's go." When they walked into Mike's department, all conversation ceased and everyone looked down at their work. As they walked through the department, no one wanted to make eye contact with Mike. Nancy saw two people roll their eyes at each other as Mike passed by. Others displayed their resentment when Mike's back was turned. It seemed as if everyone was afraid of being chewed out. Everyone looked sour or sarcastic. Nancy also noticed that Mike didn't seem all that comfortable as he walked through his department.

When they returned to Mike's office, Nancy said, "Let me start out by saying that your job as a manager is to tap into as much of the discretionary effort of your employees as possible."

"Discretionary effort—what's that?"

"Employees regulate the amount of effort they'll put into their jobs based, in large part, on how they feel they're being treated by their boss. If they feel they're being treated well, they'll give their absolute best efforts. If they feel unappreciated, they'll do only what they have to in order to hang on to their jobs. And, if they feel abused, they'll find some way to get back at their boss or they'll move on to another job."

Nancy continued, "Right now, your employees are working in an atmosphere of fear and resentment, which means they feel they're being abused. As a result, they're getting back at you—they're making sure your QPI is the worst in the company."

NEGATIVE PEOPLE ARE A LUXURY THAT MOST BUSINESSES CAN'T AFFORD

Negative people who make nasty comments to belittle or suppress those around them are a tremendous drain on the productivity of a business. The problem is that negative comments are hurtful and almost always ruin people's days. When this occurs, it immediately sucks away people's energy, and now they are no longer able to apply their best effort toward doing their job. A manager from a large company recently told us that he receives at least one degrading e-mail a month from one of his superiors. "When this happens," he said, "I completely shut down for the rest of the day." Let's assume that twenty-nine other employees received similar e-mails from that same person. If each of them responded by shutting down for a half-day, that's fifteen days of lost productivity each month—all because of one thoughtless e-mail! The message here is: If you have negative people working at your company, *especially if they're in supervisory or managerial positions*, don't ignore them. You need to find a way to get them rehabilitated or get rid of them, because they're a luxury you simply can't afford.

Mike's jaw dropped when he heard this. "Is there any way to fix this?'

"You need to replace the current atmosphere of your department with an atmosphere of trust. Once you do that, your employees will start giving you more of their discretionary effort right away."

"There has to be more to it than that."

"No, that's all you need to do, and I'll show you how." Nancy then walked over to the flip chart in the corner or Mike's office and wrote:

DESTINATION: WORK

- Focus on People as well as Performance Numbers
- Motivate with Trust Instead of Fear
    The Four Be's For Motivating With Trust
    - Be Real
    - Be Appreciative
    - Be Interested
    - Be Nice
- Turn Work into Fun

After she finished writing, Nancy took the time to explain each of the points to Mike.

After she had finished, Mike looked at her and said, "I can see why J.T. would refer to this as touchy-feely garbage."

"I hear what you are saying, Mike, but I saw the results of this method at ValuFirst Airlines. The employees were excited about what they were doing and they were working hard the whole time."

"Are you sure it will work in my department? After all, most of what we do is pretty dull and repetitive. We're talking about stuffing envelopes, metering mail, attaching labels, and packing boxes."

"Do you think issuing boarding passes and loading luggage is any less dull and repetitive?"

"I see your point, but this is going to take some getting used to. I've been hiding behind this phony 'tough boss' act for a long time. Right now, I'm not appreciative, I'm not interested in the people who work for me, and I'm not nice."

"I can tell you're not very happy either. And, like

J.T., you probably spend most of your time in your office analyzing performance numbers."

"That's right. It's no fun circulating through your department when everyone who works for you hates you. There are just too many bad vibes coming at me."

"Well, you and I are about to change all that. We're going to transform your department into a destination that people look forward to coming to each morning and giving their best efforts. We're also going to transform you into the kind of manager your employees are glad to see walking in their direction."

"How long do you think it will take before we see some results?"

"That's the beauty of this program. You'll start to see big time changes right away."

"That almost sounds too good to be true," he said doubtfully.

"Believe me, it's not," Nancy said confidently. "Look at it this way: You've got absolutely nothing to lose and everything to gain."

"You've got that right. I guess this makes us a team," he said, smiling as he shook her hand.

"You bet," said Nancy.

"How do think we should kick this thing off?"

"I suggest you have a department meeting first thing in the morning to let the people who work for you know that things are about to change in some pretty special ways. If you start trying to transform your department into a destination out of the clear blue without any explanation, they're going to think you've lost it. I also think it would be helpful if we took them over to Midway Airport to see *Destination: Work* in action at ValuFirst Airlines. Once they see what's going on and get a chance to feel the excitement, they're going to buy into the program instantly. This will also clear up any lingering doubts you might have about *Destination: Work*."

"Sounds good to me."

Nancy added, "Let me call Jack Sims, the CEO of ValuFirst, and see if I can arrange a quick tour of ValuFirst's operations at Midway."

"Do you think he'll mind us barging in like that?"

"Not at all; he told me to call him anytime. Let me go back to my office and see if I can set this up."

Twenty minutes later she returned. "I got a hold of Jack Sims and he not only agreed to take us on a tour to see *Destination: Work* in action, but he's also setting up a meeting in one of ValuFirst's conference rooms where he and several of his employees will make a presentation about the program and answer any questions. He said that he would be best for him if we showed up around noon."

"This is fantastic; that way we can use our lunch hour for part of the tour. I'll arrange for a couple of vans to take us over. Do you have any advice on what I ought to say at the meeting tomorrow morning?"

"Not really. Just keep in mind that the most important aspect of motivating with trust is to be real—be yourself and let your heart do the talking. I also think you should read this," she said as she handed Mike a copy of the report she had written for J.T. "It won't take you all that long, but I think it will make you feel a lot more confident about tomorrow."

"Thanks."

"How about if we show up a half hour early tomorrow in case you have any last-minute questions?" suggested Nancy.

"That's a great idea. See you then. . . ."

. . . . .

"Boy, J.T. sure didn't like hearing the idea about making work a destination, did he?" asked Joe.

"No he didn't. That's why I had to draw him into that bet. I was hoping that once he saw Destination: Work *in action right there at* Biz Trenz, *he would finally see the light."*

NUGGETS FROM CHAPTER 6

How can you tell if you're using fear as a motivator? The next time you walk through your department, ask yourself the following questions:

1. Do my employees look like they're glad to see me?

2. Do my employees have smiles on their faces most of the time?

3. Do my employees eagerly make eye contact with me?

4. Do I feel my employees have my best interests at heart?

If the answer to each of these questions is "no," you are using fear as a motivator. This means your department is underachieving, which is costing you on your performance review.

CHAPTER 7
GETTING THE BUY-IN

"The next morning, as I approached Mike's office, I saw him feverishly writing things down on his notepad. He told me he was really glad that he had read my report, because it took care of all the doubts he had when he left work the day before. He related that he was really eager to get started. Shortly after eight o'clock, the members of his department began filing into the conference room. They all looked stricken; more like they were being taken to the 'woodshed' than going to a departmental meeting. After everyone was seated, Mike stood up and addressed the group. . . ."

. . . . .

I **have been** your department manager for the past year and I want to be the first to point out that I've done a lousy job! I thought that being a hard-nosed manager who pointed out mistakes and then chewed people out was the way to go. Well, I was wrong and for that I want to apologize."

Everyone in the room looked shocked—they couldn't believe what they were hearing.

Mike continued as he looked at Nancy. "This is Nancy Kim who also works here at *Biz Trenz*. During this past week, she has learned of a method of managing that is far superior to anything I've ever heard of before. It's called *Destination: Work* and it's built around the fact that *you* are this department's most important resource. Further, it replaces the atmosphere of fear, which has charac-terized this department since I've been here, with an atmosphere of trust. It also changes my role from being someone who points out mistakes and chews people out to being someone whose primary job is to support you. I spent most of last night studying it and I'm convinced it will work, so I want to give it a try. I also want you to give it a try."

"Mike, are you okay?" asked Ken.

"Did you just get a bad diagnosis from your doctor?" asked an employee named Jay.

The room then burst into laughter.

"Let me put it this way: I think I've finally seen the light. I think this department is full of great people who are capable of some really great things—like taking our QPI to a nine or above—if we work together and I do an effective job of supporting you."

"Can you tell us a little more about *Destination: Work*?" asked a woman named Jeannie.

"You bet!" said Nancy. "The goal is to make this department a destination—a place where everyone is excited about coming to work every day. But rather than tell you about it, Mike and I would like to show it to you firsthand. So, at eleven forty-five this morning two vans are going to pick us up in front of the Visitor's Lobby and take us to Midway Airport."

"Why are we going to Midway? Are you taking us to Disneyworld too?" joked Ken.

"No, no Disneyworld this time. We're going to take a tour of ValuFirst Airlines. They're the most profitable airline in the industry and *Destination: Work* is the management program they use."

"My friend works there," said Jeannie, "and she absolutely loves it. She can't wait to go to work in the morning."

"My sister works there," said Marci. "She says it's the most fun place to work that you could ever imagine."

"This sounds exciting," said Jay. "I must admit that I have been thinking about looking for a job somewhere else, but now I'm going to stick around to see what happens. I have flown ValuFirst a number of times and have always been impressed about how excited and happy its employees seemed to be."

"It will be exciting," said Nancy, "and Jack Sims, the CEO of ValuFirst, will personally lead us on the tour, then make a presentation about his

Destination: Work program and answer questions about it afterward."

"I'm impressed," said Ken. "Jack Sims is one of the most famous business executives in the world."

"Okay then," said Nancy, "we'll see you out front at eleven forty-five."

There was a lot of enthusiastic chatter as the employees of Mike's department filed out of the conference room door to go back to work. "I think we got their attention," said Mike. "They seem really excited about where all this is going."

"Just wait until you see how they behave *after* the tour," Nancy said smiling. . . .

At noon, Nancy led her entourage into the ValuFirst ticketing area where Jack Sims waited. He greeted each person as he handed out temporary security badges. He then gave everyone a small notepad and pen and asked them to record their observations while they were on the tour.

He took them on pretty much the same tour as he had taken Nancy. They spent about twenty minutes in the ticketing area and then went through security into the gate area. The final phase of the tour involved going to the top level of the parking structure where they could watch planes coming into and departing from a number of ValuFirst gates. Here Jack broke the group into three subgroups and asked each to pick out a different plane and note how long it took the plane to make a turnaround at the gate. All three took less than twenty minutes and everyone, including Mike, stood in awe as they watched.

Afterward, they assembled in a conference room. In front of the room were Jack and five other ValuFirst employees. Jack opened the meeting by asking the group what observations they had recorded in their notepads. At this point everyone wanted to talk at once.

"The level of teamwork was unbelievable," said Marci, "especially when they were unloading and reloading the planes."

"I felt a sense of excitement the minute I walked into the ticket area," said Jay. "Also, I couldn't believe how fast the lines moved."

Then Ken, one of the more outspoken members of the group, raised his hand and said, "No company can pay people enough money to work that hard. There's something going on here and I would like to know what it is."

"You're absolutely right, something is going on here, and it's something very special that we would love to share with you," Jack said as he flipped open a whiteboard with the following written on it:

DESTINATION: WORK

- Focus on People as Well as Performance Numbers
- Motivate with Trust Instead of Fear
  The Four Be's For Motivating With Trust
  - Be Real
  - Be Appreciative
  - Be Interested
  - Be Nice
- Turn Work into Fun

Jack explained how they had turned working at ValuFirst into a destination by focusing on people instead of performance numbers and by motivating with trust instead of fear. When it came to the Four Be's, a different ValuFirst employee explained each one of them. A senior vice president explained Being Real, a supervisor explained Being Appreciative, a mechanic explained Being Interested, and a baggage handler explained Being Nice.

A flight attendant named Liz then explained the "Turn Work into Fun" part of *Destination: Work.* She told them how working in an atmosphere of trust allowed them to be themselves and turn their work into fun. She then gave them an example of how they manage to have fun while giving a safety briefing, saying, "In the event of a sudden loss of cabin pressure, first of all, stop screaming! Next, let go of your neighbor's arm. Then reach up and pull one of the oxygen masks that have just dropped down from the compartment above your head toward you and secure it firmly around your nose and mouth."

Later she said, "In the event this flight turns into a cruise, your life jacket is located in a plastic bag under your seat." She concluded with, "This flight is a nonsmoking flight, but once we reach our cruising altitude, we will open our smoking section, which is out on the wing. Our motto is: If you can light it, you can smoke it!" At this point, everyone was laughing. The group responded with an enthusiastic applause.

At this point, Ken asked, "Are things really that good around here, or are you just saying all these wonderful things because Jack is in the room?"

Liz responded, "Every day is a wonderful day at ValuFirst and if Jack happens to come around, things are even better. You see, Jack isn't an authority figure around here, he's one of us. He likes to have fun just like we do and, as you all know, fun is contagious."

Jeannie asked, "Does this mean that if we do those things necessary to make our department a destination, we can enjoy the same kind of success and have the same kind of fun that you experience at ValuFirst?"

"You bet!"

Then Mike stood up and said, "I'd like to see a show of hands. Is anyone here interested in making our department a destination?" Instantly, everyone's hand went up. "Then let's get started!"

On the way out of the conference room, everyone from Mike's department tried to shake as many of the ValuFirst employees' hands as possible and everyone wanted to shake hands with Jack.

"Thanks again," Nancy said as she shook Jack's hand.

"As I said before, call me anytime."

On the way back to *Biz Trenz,* both vans rocked with excitement. The people in Mike's department couldn't wait to put *Destination: Work* into action. . . .

. . . . .

"It sounds like things got off to a very good start,"
said Tom.

"Yes, they did. Jack really knows how to sell
Destination: Work.

NUGGETS FROM CHAPTER 7

Implementing *Destination: Work* makes your job as a manager easier and more fun:

1. Your employees like you and are looking out for your best interest.

2. Your employees want to talk to you and let you know what's going on.

3. Spending time with your employees becomes a source of happiness.

4. Your performance numbers go way up, which make you look really good on your performance review.

CHAPTER 8
THE MISSING STEP

"When we got back to Biz Trenz, everyone
went back to their job with a newfound sense
of optimism and enthusiasm. Mike spent the
rest of the day out in his department executing
Destination: Work. Toward the end of the day,
I looked out across the department and noticed
that all the sour looks I had seen the day before
had been replaced with smiles. I also noticed that
the level of activity had picked up considerably
and that Mike actually seemed to be enjoying
himself. Late Friday afternoon, the report that
listed each department's QPI score was published
and distributed. After Mike read the report, he

walked over to me to share the news. He was very excited. . . ."

. . . . .

"Can you believe it? My department's score has already jumped to a 5.5!"

"That's fantastic, Mike. Would you mind if I asked you a couple of quick questions?"

"Not at all, go right ahead."

"How much time did you spend in your office analyzing performance numbers these past three days?"

"Almost none."

"Where did you spend your time?"

"Out in my department with my employees."

"Tell me, are you having fun?"

"You bet. I haven't had this much fun as a manager—ever."

"And look what happened to your performance numbers."

"They went up significantly, and we've only had

Destination: Work in place for a little more than three days!"

During the ensuing weeks, Mike continued to execute *Destination: Work* and his QPI score continued to climb. Five weeks later, his department's score had reached 8.4. "We're getting close," he said as he showed the report to Nancy.

"We sure are. It shouldn't be long now before we hit 9," she said confidently.

Much to their surprise, the next week's score came in at 8.2. The following week's score was 8.3, and the one after that was 8.1.

"I can't figure it out," said Mike as he paced back and forth in his office on Thursday morning. "I'm doing the same things I've done these past nine weeks, but my department's QPI score has stopped going up. Wait a minute!" he said, experiencing an "aha" moment. "During the past nine weeks, our QPI score has been as high as an 8.4. That's a 280 percent increase from where we started. That should be enough to turn any CEO's head, but J.T. hasn't stopped by the department once to say thank you."

"You're right," said Nancy. "And by not doing so, he's sending a clear message to your employees that he doesn't appreciate what they've accomplished. This has had a demotivating effect on them and has caused them to cut back on the amount of discretionary effort they're willing to put into their jobs."

"When you think about it, his not coming by and saying thank you is actually interfering with my ability to get the most out of my employees. On the other hand, if J.T. did come by and express his appreciation, that would boost the trust level to the point where my employees would get excited about putting forth the effort required to take our QPI to a nine or above."

"You're absolutely right, I think it's time I paid old J.T. a visit."

When Nancy arrived at J.T.'s office, she found him sitting in front of his computer monitor analyzing performance numbers. "Come on in. Say, I notice the QPI for Mike's department has gone up a great deal."

"It sure has."

"But it's nowhere near the nine you need to win our bet," he said with a smirk.

"That's what I'm here to talk to you about," said Nancy. "You see the QPI of Mike's department has flattened out during these past three weeks in the high eights. Four weeks ago, they hit 8.4—which is a 280 percent increase from where they started. What Mike and I are asking you to do is to come over to his department and tell the people who work there how much you appreciate the fact that they've come such a long way in such a short period of time. We think your doing so would motivate them to apply the effort necessary to take their QPI to a nine or above."

"Look, you know it's not my style to praise progress—I only praise end results. When Mike's department reaches a QPI of nine or above, I'll come over and say thank you, but not until then."

"I think your missing the point, J.T., by not coming over and acknowledging their progress, you're telling the people in Mike's department that you don't appreciate what they've accomplished. This has a demotivating effect, which is causing them to cut back on the amount of discretionary effort they're willing to apply to their jobs. If you come over and acknowledge their progress, they **will** hit a nine or above."

"Oh, so you're trying to blame me for Mike's department's not being able to get its QPI up to a nine. Now I've heard everything. Case closed," he said as he turned back to his computer monitor, "case closed."

Nancy was upset as she walked back to Mike's office. She thought, *Why does J.T. have to be so pigheaded? After all, he's the one who's ultimately going to benefit from all of this.*

When she arrived at the department, Mike could tell she wasn't very happy. "What did J.T. have to say?"

"Basically, that he wouldn't say or do anything until your department hit a score of nine or above."

"We should have expected as much."

"I suppose you're right on that one, but where do we go from here?"

HUMILITY AND RECOGNIZING OTHERS—HALLMARKS OF A GREAT LEADER

Author Jim Collins conducted research on leaders who were able to take their respective companies from being "good" to being "great." As a result, he was able to identify some of the characteristics these leaders had in common. First, these leaders possessed extreme personal humility. Even though they were running the company, they were not arrogant, condescending, or otherwise taken with themselves. Second, they gave away all the credit to others when things went well and they absorbed all the blame when things went poorly. So, keep this in mind the next time you're tempted to get on your "high horse" or point fingers at someone—it's not what great leaders do.

"I think we need to pay another visit to Jack Sims."

"I think you're right."

Nancy called Jack. "Hello, Jack? It's Nancy. I was wondering if Mike and I could spend a little time with you again, preferably tomorrow, if you have time. It's a rather urgent problem."

"Sure. Why don't you come out to the house around two?"

"That would be great. Thank you so much."

"I'll see you tomorrow. . . ."

At two o'clock on Friday afternoon, Nancy and Mike were sitting in Jack's home office. "So, tell me, what can I do for you?" he asked.

Nancy told him about the bet with J.T. and about the early success they had implementing *Destination: Work* in Mike's department. She also mentioned how the department's QPI had leveled off in recent weeks. Mike then shared how J.T. refused to come over to his department and say thank you for what he thought was pretty amazing progress in a fairly short time. Jack listened intently as the two spoke.

"I guess I have two questions," said Nancy. "First, is it really that important that the senior managers in a company, including the CEO, execute *Destination: Work* with frontline employees? And if it is, how do we get J.T. to embrace the program?"

"Allow me to answer those two questions in order," said Jack as he went to his whiteboard. "What you've done is discovered the fourth and final step of our *Destination: Work* program. I didn't give it to you the last time you were here because I wanted you to discover it on your own. That way you would better appreciate how important it is." Jack then added the fourth step, which he underlined:

DESTINATION: WORK

- Focus on People as Well as
  Performance Numbers
- Motivate with Trust Instead of Fear
  The Four Be's For Motivating With Trust
  - Be Real
  - Be Appreciative
  - Be Interested
  - Be Nice
- Turn Work Into Fun
- Senior Management Must Execute
  Destination: Work with Frontline Employees

"In order for a manager to get the most discretionary effort from his or her employees, it's of paramount importance that the managers and executives above him or her support the effort by embracing *Destination: Work* and executing it with frontline employees. Probably, the biggest single mistake senior managers make is that they don't positively interact with these people on a regular basis."

"Why is that?"

"They don't see the need because they don't understand that their not interacting with frontline employees sends a very clear message that they don't care about them. Employees respond to this by cutting back on the amount of discretionary effort they are willing to apply to their jobs."

"This not only takes its toll on the performance numbers and bottom line that these senior managers are so preoccupied with," said Nancy, "it also makes the job of the subordinate managers that much more difficult."

LANDMARK STUDY REVEALS THAT SENIOR MANAGEMENT HAS A FAR GREATER IMPACT ON DISCRETIONARY EFFORT THAN AN EMPLOYEE'S IMMEDIATE BOSS

It's a long held belief that the immediate boss has the most influence over how much discretionary effort an employee is willing to apply toward his or her job. Towers Perrin in their *Global Workforce Study,* which included nearly 90,000 workers from eighteen countries, found this not to be true. The study found that while the impact of the immediate boss is large, the top single driver of discretionary effort is "senior management's sincere interest in employee well being." In other words, does senior management consistently demonstrate that it truly cares about frontline employees? The study goes on to say: "Senior managers now know that it is not enough for them to observe the significance of employee engagement (willingness to apply discretionary effort) from afar and then task their HR and line managers to do something about it. They themselves represent part of the problem, and a major part of the solution." The study indicates that senior management could significantly increase levels of employee discretionary effort ". . . by doing a few simple things sincerely, consistently, and well. In order of importance the top three of these are:

1. Communicate openly and honestly
2. Be visible and accessible
3. Show support for new ideas."

The study also points out that senior management's function as role models for managers throughout the organization cannot be overestimated. "Their interest in staff, even if demonstrated in small ways, will be carefully noted by others lower down the management structure."

"That's right. On the other hand, when senior managers do positively interact with frontline employees, those employees will put every bit of discretionary effort they have toward performing their jobs. As a frontline worker, nothing is more exciting than to have the company CEO or some other senior manager come through your department and pat you on the back and either saying 'thank you' or something like, 'Let me take over your job for a while, while you take a break,' or having him or her working right alongside you for a while talking to you about whatever."

Jack continued, "Let me tell you about a few of the things I do as the CEO at ValuFirst. I always make it a point to spend a full shift loading baggage on the day before the Thanksgiving holiday. Why? Because I want my employees to know that I know how hard it is to do their job on the busiest travel day of the year. I do the same thing on Christmas Day, because I want those employees to know that I know firsthand what it's like to have to work on a very special holiday. I also regularly come to work at midnight at different airports around the country dressed in coveralls and carrying a box of dough-nuts to help the cleaning crews clean the planes. I want these employees to know that as their CEO, I don't consider myself too good to do the dirty work that needs to be done. In addition, every one of my managers is required to spend one-third of their time out among their employees—not pointing out mistakes or giving orders, but working right along-side them executing *Destination: Work.*"

SENIOR MANAGERS NEED TO GET INVOLVED WITH FRONTLINE EMPLOYEES

Recently, **Business Week** published its ranking of the top twenty-five providers of customer service. As it turns out, these companies have two things in common: First, they consider their employees at least as important, if not more so, as their customers and treat them accordingly. Second, the senior management of these companies spends lots and lots of time out on the frontlines doing things like listening to phone conversations at the call center or working alongside frontline employees delivering the service. As the article put it, "While treating your employees right and staying close to the frontlines may sound like simplistic platitudes, they are the hard truth about the hard work of getting service right." Unfortunately, this is one of those truths that so many senior managers fail to "get" as many of them choose to spend their time as far away from the frontlines as they can. On the other hand, those that do, like the senior managers at USAA, Nordstrom, Starbuck's, and Southwest Airlines, consistently have their companies performing like champions.

"I'll bet your employees have a lot of respect for you for doing these things."

"Yes, they do. But more importantly, they know that I respect and care about them—that's what gets them excited about putting all their discretionary effort into their jobs, which is what makes ValuFirst so successful."

Jack continued, "There's one other very important thing to keep in mind here."

"What's that?" asked Nancy.

"Team leaders, supervisors, and managers tend to model the behavior of the managers above them. If they see senior managers positively interacting with frontline employees, they are far more likely to do it themselves. This is why *Destination: Work* has been such a long-term success here at ValuFirst. On the other hand, if team leaders, supervisors, and managers don't see the managers above them positively interacting with frontline employees, they eventually conclude that it must not be all that important, so they stop doing it. When this happens, employees pull back on the amount of discretionary effort they're willing to put into their jobs and productivity takes a big hit."

"What you're saying is that if senior managers don't embrace *Destination: Work* and regularly execute it with frontline employees, it has no chance of surviving over the long term."

"It's a scary thought, isn't it?"

"I'll say," said Nancy. "Now let's move on to my second question. How do we get J.T. to execute *Destination: Work* in Mike's department?"

"Under normal circumstances, I would say that getting someone like J.T. to change his attitude and embrace *Destination: Work* would be close to impossible, but I think I just might have an ace up my sleeve."

"What do you mean?"

"I loaned J.T. the money to start *Biz Trenz* when none of the banks would. He was so grateful that he told me if I ever needed a favor from him, no matter how large, that I shouldn't hesitate to ask. I would never think of collecting on such a promise, but since J.T. is ultimately going to benefit from em-bracing this program, I think it's time I called in the favor. Nancy, why don't you see if you can get him on my speaker phone? This is going to be fun."

"Hello, J.T., this is Nancy."

"What's up?"

"I'm on a speaker phone with an old friend of yours who wants to say hi."

"J.T., this is Jack Sims."

"Why Jack, you old rattlesnake, how are you?"

"I'm great, thank you. The reason I'm calling is to ask you for a favor."

"Anything you ask."

"On Monday, I would like you to go over to Mike's department and pat his employees on the back for coming such a long way on their QPI rating in such a short time. I also want you to embrace a program called *Destination: Work* and execute it in Mike's department for the next two weeks."

"But Jack, I can't do that. I know about your *Destination: Work* program because I read about it in a report Nancy wrote after she visited with you.

No offense, Jack, but as far as I'm concerned, it's nothing but a touchy-feely gimmick."

"J.T., I developed that program and that's the way we manage at ValuFirst from the very top on, down. I'm sure you're aware how successful my airline has been."

"I know it's a lot more profitable than *Biz Trenz*."

"Then do we have a deal?"

"It would be a lot less painful if you asked me to buy you a Jaguar or a house on the lake."

"Well then, let me sweeten the pot a little. All I want you to do is to spend ten minutes a day in Mike's department executing *Destination: Work*. If at the end of the two weeks, you're still convinced it's nothing but a touchy-feely gimmick, I'll give you and your wife lifetime travel passes on ValuFirst."

"Now you're talking, Jack. But keep in mind, when you lose this bet, I intend to collect those travel passes."

"Then it's a deal?"

"You bet! Nancy, I'd like to see you and Mike

in my office on Monday morning at seven o'clock. We've got to plan this thing out so I don't wind up looking like a first-class fool."

"Will do. . . ."

. . . . .

"Jack turned out to be quite an ally in your quest to change the work environment at Biz Trenz," *said Tom.*

"Did he ever! I was so glad he had that ace up his sleeve, because I don't know how I would have gotten J.T. to go out into Mike's department and give Destination: Work *a try."*

NUGGETS FROM CHAPTER 8

**When senior managers embrace *Destination:
Work* and interact with frontline employees,
they get the message that senior management really does care about them. When this
occurs, some very wonderful things start to
happen:**

1. Frontline employees apply even more of their
   discretionary effort toward performing their
   jobs.

2. The jobs of subordinate managers become
   much easier because senior management is
   directly supporting their efforts.

3. Performance numbers and the bottom line
   go to the next level.

CHAPTER 9
STEPPING OUTSIDE
THE COMFORT ZONE

"As Mike and I entered J.T.'s office on Monday morning, we found him frantically pacing the floor. When J.T. looked up and saw us he said, 'This is a fine mess you've got me into. I didn't sleep a bit last night! Nancy, I reread your report several times after dinner. Then, when I finally went to bed, I kept hearing this voice say over and over, focus on people instead of numbers. Several times I broke out in a cold sweat. Then I started mulling over different ways of carrying out Destination: Work in Mike's department. The next thing I knew, it was morning.' I told J.T. to relax; that everything was going to be fine. . . ."

. . . . .

"That's easy** for you to say! This is the most preposterous thing I've ever done—it goes against everything I believe and stand for. But I'm a man of my word and I intend to see this thing through, come hell or high water. Besides, my wife has her heart set on those lifetime travel passes."

"J.T., I think you're in for some very pleasant surprises."

"Yeah, right! Surprises, maybe, but pleasant, I don't think so."

J.T. then shared his outline regarding how he was going to thank the people in Mike's department for the vast improvement they made in the department's QPI score. He also shared with them a list of the different ways in which he was going to Be Appreciative, Be Interested, and Be Nice. "I have to admit, the Be Real part really threw me. But as I was leaving the house this morning my wife suggested that I simply behave at work the way I do around her and our friends. So, what do you touchy-feely experts think?"

T. J.'S LIST

Be Real
- Behave the same way around employees as I do around family and friends—treat them as equals, not as subordinates.

Be Appreciative
- Let employees know how happy I am that they work at *Biz Trendz*
- Make a point to notice when an employee is doing a super job and be sure to tell them "thank you."

Be Interested
- Ask employees questions about them and their jobs
  - Listen to what they say.
  - Ask follow-up questions.
  - Don't talk about yourself.

Be Nice
- Smile
- Say something that brightens each person's day:
  - A cheerful "hello!"
  - Ask "How are you doing today?"
  - "I really appreciate your cheerful attitude."

"It looks like you have a plan, J.T."

"Well then, let's get this show on the road. Mike, why don't you go on ahead and call a department meeting. Nancy and I will be along in a few minutes."

"Will do, J.T."

When they arrived at the conference room, everyone in Mike's department was waiting. Mike then said, "I'd like to introduce our CEO, J.T. He has some things he'd like to say to you."

"During the past nearly ten weeks, you folks have made an incredible improvement in your department's QPI score. This used to be one of the worst departments at *Biz Trenz* and now it's one of the best. For that, I, as the CEO, say thank you. Such an accomplishment is a direct reflection of the caliber of each person who works here as well as the quality of the department manager. Believe me, I wish we had more success stories like yours to brag about here at *Biz Trenz*. During the next several weeks, I plan to spend a little time in your department to find out exactly what is going on so that we can try to clone your amazing success in some of our other departments. Once again, thank you so much for a job extremely well done!"

The room broke into applause as Nancy and Mike looked at each other in disbelief. Everyone stood in line to shake J.T.'s hand before they left the room. In the middle of all this, J.T. noticed that he felt particularly good about what was happening. After everyone else had left the room, he walked over to where Nancy and Mike were standing and said, "Well, how did I do on my maiden voyage into touchy-feely land?"

Nancy was initially at a loss for words. Finally she said, "You were awesome, J.T., just awesome!"

"You sounded like a native of touchy-feely land," said Mike

J.T. smiled, obviously pleased with the way things had transpired. "I've got to make a few phone calls right now, but I'll be back later."

When Nancy and Mike walked out into Mike's department, they noticed everyone working with a renewed sense of excitement. "I have to admit that old J.T. really inspired these people with his expression of gratitude," said Mike.

"He sure did. Either that was a superb job of acting on his part, or he's starting to see the light."

"For some strange reason, I get the feeling he wasn't acting, but we'll see."

When Nancy and Mike returned from lunch, they noticed J.T. sitting next to Jeannie. The two were stuffing envelopes and chatting away. The next morning, when she arrived at Mike's department, they saw J.T. getting some pointers from Ken on how to fill out a customs form for international shipping. Later that day, she found him printing out labels while a young man named Guy, whose job it was, looked on smiling.

Late that afternoon as she was on her way home, Jeannie stopped by Mike's office where he was talking with Nancy. "Correct me if I'm wrong, but didn't the two of you tell me a while back that J.T. was an insensitive hard-nosed CEO?"

"Yes we did," said Nancy.

"Well, I've got to tell you from firsthand

experience, the guy is a real hoot. He's actually a lot of fun to be around. Is there any chance the two of you may have misjudged him?"

"That's a distinct possibility," said Nancy, with a sheepish grin. "Have a nice evening, Jeannie, and thanks for stopping by."

Throughout the rest of the week, J.T. continued to come over to Mike's department at least once a day. When he was there, he always smiled and had something positive to say to everyone he talked to. When others talked, he listened and he never missed an opportunity to pat someone on the back or thank them for something. When the QPI ratings were published on Friday afternoon, Mike's department came in at an 8.9.

"We're almost there," Nancy said to Mike as they were leaving work. "Next week is when it's going to happen."

"I sure hope so, have a great weekend."

"You too, Mike. . . ."

On Monday morning, when Nancy and Mike arrived at Mike's department, J.T. was already there handing out doughnuts and congratulating the people on last week's big jump in the department's QPI score. The members of Mike's department were all smiling and glad to see him. J.T. was thoroughly enjoying his new role. During the rest of the week, J.T. came through the department at least once a day to, as he put it, "practice *Destination: Work.*" He could hardly keep himself away because he so enjoyed the good feelings he got there.

As usual, the report listing each department's QPI scores was released late Friday afternoon. When Nancy and Mike looked at it, they were stunned. The score for Mike's department was a 7.9! "How could that have happened?" asked Mike. "I thought all week that things were moving along perfectively."

"I know," said Nancy, "I thought for sure you were going to get way beyond nine."

Just then Mike's phone rang. It was J.T. "Say Mike, I just saw your department's QPI score. I would like you to call a departmental meeting so we can talk about it—this is serious business. I'll be over in ten minutes."

"Alright J.T., see you in a few."

"What's up?" asked Nancy

"J.T. wants me to call a departmental meeting so he can come over and talk about our QPI score. I don't think he's happy with it."

As J.T. entered the conference room, he noticed that each person there looked dejected. Then J.T. spoke with a serious expression on his face. "Nearly two weeks ago, I came to this conference room to congratulate you for having made incredible progress in elevating your department's QPI score. Today I'm afraid I'm going to have to take all of that back."

J.T. continued as the mood in the room grew somber. "First of all, the score that was printed in the weekly report was incorrect. It was printed incorrectly on purpose so that I could come here in person to see the expressions on your faces when I told you that you're true score is a 9.8—the highest in the history of *Biz Trenz*! This no longer qualifies as incredible progress, it qualifies as **unbelievable** progress! You've just set the standard for the rest of *Biz Trenz*. As your CEO, I would like to offer my heartiest congratulations to all of you."

The room burst into applause. Just then, the door to the conference room opened and in walked a woman carrying a huge cake. J.T. shouted, "My wife, Susan, baked this cake so that we could celebrate your wonderful achievement, so let's get started!" At this point, people started passing around "high fives" and hugging each other—and J.T. was right in the middle of it all.

After the celebrating had calmed, Nancy walked over to J.T. and said, "You seem incredibly happy for someone who just lost a bet."

"Let me tell you, it's the best bet I've ever lost! These past two weeks have been a life-changing experience for me. I have to admit that I've never enjoyed being a CEO more. I now understand what you wrote in your report about tapping into the discretionary effort of our employees. Embracing

CELEBRATE YOUR SUCCESSES

When you achieve something that's important to you, don't let the moment pass without celebrating. Achievements always involve the expenditure of extra effort over an extended period of time and often involve some disappointment, frustration, setbacks, and burnout. Celebrating these moments is what recharges your batteries so you can go out there and conquer new challenges. Not celebrating these occasions is to deprive yourself of a much needed infusion of positive energy. Most people don't celebrate enough. They tend to dwell on the things that didn't work out rather than focus on the things that did, which drains them of energy. So, the next time you achieve something, no matter how small, pull a few friends together and savor the moment. Doing so will provide a springboard toward your next important achievement.

Destination: Work is the kind of thing I should have been doing all along instead of sitting in front of my computer analyzing performance numbers. I want you to know that I'm going to publish that report of yours, just like you wrote it, as the cover story in the next issue of *Biz Trenz*."

"You seem like a changed man, J.T. What was it that made you change?" asked Nancy.

"As you know, I've always been a performance numbers and bottom-line CEO. But you really got my attention when you said that if I implemented my **Management by the Numbers** program, eventually the only people working here will be those who can't get jobs anywhere else. You went on to say, 'If you think productivity is bad now, just watch how bad it gets after all our good employees have left.' I couldn't get that idea out of my head—it was a very sobering thought. I knew then that we had to start doing things differently at *Biz Trenz*, but I didn't know what. Then I watched what you and Mike were able to accomplish literally over-night. Let me tell you, that 280 percent increase of the department's QPI score in just six weeks is one amazing turnaround. At that point I knew I needed to start focusing more on our employees and less on performance numbers, even though doing so was way outside my comfort zone."

"I'd be curious to know what went through your mind when our QPI score leveled off in the low eights?"

"Well, I knew something was missing and I have to admit that I had no idea what it was. But I knew if I kept up the pressure by reminding you of our bet, that you'd eventually figure it out."

"J.T., I can't believe you were stringing us along like that."

"Let's just say it was for a good cause," he said, smiling.

"Did it bother you that Jack Sims called in his marker on that promise you made to him when he loaned you the money to start *Biz Trenz*?"

"Not at all. That made it look like I was going along with your little escapade against my will. It made the whole adventure a great deal of fun for me—seeing those perplexed looks on your faces when it looked to you like I was enjoying what I was doing."

"I remember on that Monday morning when we kicked this thing off, I said that you were in for some pleasant surprises. Well, J.T., you really turned the tables on us, because we were the ones who experienced all the surprises."

"Well, there was one very positive surprise for me. I had no idea how huge of an impact that a CEO's occasionally interacting with frontline employees could have on a department's performance."

"That truly *is* the most important thing that most CEOs and senior managers don't seem to understand," said Nancy. "When Mike, as the department manager, executed *Destination: Work* with his employees, the performance results were incredible. But when you, as the CEO, did it too, they went through the roof."

"Amen," said J.T. Then he shouted, "I have an announcement to make! Throughout the history of

KEEPING YOUR HANDS "DIRTY" AS AN EXECUTIVE OR MANAGER SUSTAINS YOUR SUCCESS

Many people, once they get promoted into the executive or managerial ranks, mistakenly assume that they're all done getting their hands dirty—doing the nitty-gritty day-to-day menial jobs on the frontline. A recent study of highly successful companies reported in **Fast Company** magazine points out that quite the opposite is true. In these companies, the CEOs required their executives and managers to spend a fair amount of their time doing frontline work—not pointing out mistakes or giving out orders, but working right alongside the frontline employees. Doing this not only keeps you in touch with the "nuts and bolts" of your business and your customers, but it also lets the frontline employees know that you understand how hard it is to do their job. This sends a very clear message that you, as the manager, respect what they do. This not only energizes the frontline employees, it greatly increases the amount of respect they have for you as their manager.

our company, we have never had an executive vice president. Well, I want you to know that we have one now and her name is Nancy Kim!"

The room broke into a thunderous ovation. When the room quieted down, J.T. continued, "Her full-time job will be to see to it that *Destination: Work* is implemented in every department at *Biz Trenz.* . . ."

. . . . .

"What a wonderful story," said Max.

"I'll second that," said Tom.

"Your story also illustrates that there is no patented formula for getting senior management to embrace a program like Destination: Work *even though they're the ones who are ultimately going to benefit from it," said Joe.*

"That's probably true," said Nancy.
"Confronting them with the facts doesn't work. As Max pointed out earlier, we've known since the 1920s that paying positive attention to the

*people who work for you has a dominant impact
on their productivity, but no one seems to care.
Logic doesn't work either—everyone pretty much
understands that the better you treat employees,
the harder they'll work, but almost no one is
willing to do anything about it. It's definitely
a hard sell even though it should be one of the
easiest."*

*"And you can't always count on people like
Jack Sims, who just happen to have an ace up
their sleeve," said Freddie.*

*"No, you can't, but you can issue a
nonthreatening challenge like I did with J.T.—get
senior management to let you try* Destination:
Work *in a single department that is performing
poorly."*

"Isn't that kind of risky?" asked Tom.

*"Not really. Anytime you implement a
program like* Destination: Work *in a poorly
performing department, it's virtually guaranteed
that productivity will turn around quickly and
dramatically, because that's the kind of work*

environment employees thrive in. Once a CEO or senior executive sees how hard employees are willing to work if they're treated right, it's like a lightbulb goes on in their brain—they start to see how they would benefit personally if Destination: Work *were implemented across the entire company. Remember, the instant turnaround that took place in Mike's department caught J.T.'s attention long before he let on. When this happens, there's no turning back. They become evangelists for the program."*

"Is this what happened to J.T.?" asked Freddie.

"I suppose it's time to finish my story."

NUGGETS FROM CHAPTER 9

When a company embraces *Destination: Work*, everybody wins:

1. Employees look forward to coming to work and working hard.

2. Lower and middle managers no longer have to worry about their performance reviews.

3. The performance numbers and bottom line that senior managers are so concerned with far exceed anything that would have been possible through managing strictly by the numbers.

4. The entire workplace is characterized by contagious excitement, which translates into positive experiences for customers and shareholders.

CHAPTER 10
SEAMLESS EXCELLENCE

"I took my new job seriously. In no time at all, everyone at Biz Trenz, *including upper management, embraced* Destination: Work *and was actively executing it. Work at* Biz Trenz *had indeed become a destination. This set the stage for unprecedented growth and profitability—so much so, that the business community quickly took notice. J.T. was being invited to speak to executive groups all over the country about the secrets behind* Biz Trenz's *amazing turnaround. Whenever he delivered one of these speeches, he would always say, 'If you want to experience the*

same level of success that we've achieved at Biz Trenz, you have to make your frontline employees your top priority. If you treat them right, they'll work hard and they'll treat your customers right. And if your customers feel they're being treated right, they'll not only come back again and again but they'll tell others about their wonderful experiences—and this, my fellow executives, is what creates value for your shareholders.' We refer to this at Biz Trenz as **Seamless Excellence.**"

"*It sounds like things worked out really well for you, Nancy,*" said Joe.

"*They sure did; even better than you know.*"

"*What do you mean?*" asked Freddie.

"*Spending all that time with Jack, rekindled our relationship—Jack is widowed also. Freddie, I think you and I need to talk. . . .*"

NUGGETS FROM CHAPTER 10

Destination: Work is the best bargain on the planet:

1. It costs nothing.

2. It requires almost no effort.

3. It drives performance numbers and the bottom line through the roof.

4. The impact is instant.

5. Everybody wins.

PUTTING *DESTINATION:*
WORK INTO ACTION

DESTINATION: WORK

Daily Execution Guidelines

<u>GOAL</u>: To turn work into a destination—a place that employees are excited about coming to every day.

———

<u>STEP ONE</u>: Focus on people as well as performance numbers.

Employees regulate the amount of effort they're willing to put into their jobs based upon how they feel they're being treated. Your job as a manager is to treat them in such a way that they become excited about applying all their discretionary effort toward performing their jobs.

———

<u>STEP TWO</u>: You bring out the best in people by motivating with trust instead of fear.

Be Real—Be yourself and let the real you shine through.

KEY BEHAVIORS:

1. Be nice because you care, not because you want something.

2. Don't try to come across as someone who is superior to your employees. Instead, reach out and embrace them as equals.

Be Appreciative—People absolutely love to work hard when their efforts are noticed and appreciated by their boss.

KEY BEHAVIORS:

1. Make it a point to notice all the things your employees do on your behalf.

2. Then thank them in a way that is meaningful to them.

Remember, nothing is more demotivating than going the extra mile and having your boss not notice or care.

Be Interested—Treat your employees like they really are your most important resource. After all, it's their level of effort that determines your success.

KEY BEHAVIORS:

1. Regularly circulate among your employees.

2. Let them get to know you.

3. Ask their opinion on things.

4. Listen to what they have to say.

5. Take action when appropriate.

Be Nice—This is what makes people like you and they have to like you before they can trust you.

KEY BEHAVIORS:

1. Smile.

2. Say or do something that brightens each person's day.

<u>STEP THREE</u>: Turn work into fun.

When you're having fun, what you're doing never becomes old or boring.

KEY BEHAVIORS:

1. Be a role model for your employees by having fun yourself and being a fun person to be around.

2. Encourage your employees to express their uniqueness.

<u>STEP FOUR</u>: Senior management must execute *Destination: Work* with frontline employees.

The Towers Perrin **Global Workforce Study** found that the top single driver of discretionary effort is "senior management's sincere interest in employee well being." Therefore, an extremely important part of your job is to support the efforts of your subordinate managers by embracing *Destination: Work* and executing it with frontline employees.

KEY BEHAVIORS:

1. Regularly circulate among frontline employees while executing the Four Be's.

2. Jump into the trenches, on a regular basis, and work alongside frontline employees to show that you respect and care about them.

A NOTE FOR SENIOR MANAGERS

Remember, nothing is more exciting to a frontline employee than to have the company CEO or some other senior manager come through the department and personally interact with him or her. If you take the time to positively interact with frontline employees on a regular basis, those employees will apply every bit of discretionary effort they have toward performing their jobs.

Also remember that team leaders, supervisors, and managers tend to model the behavior of the managers above them. If they see senior management positively interacting with frontline employees, they are far more likely to do it themselves. This is what gives *Destination: Work* its staying power over the long term. On the other hand, if team leaders, supervisors, and managers don't see senior management positively interacting with frontline employees, they eventually conclude that it must not be all that important, so they stop doing it. When this happens, employees pull back on the amount of discretionary effort they're willing to put into their jobs, productivity takes a big hit, and *Destination: Work* becomes a thing of the past.

ACKNOWLEDGMENTS

There are many people involved in getting a book ready for publication, and we feel that there are several that we must single out.

Marcia Reck, Ross's wife, for her willingness to proofread on demand throughout the duration of this project.

Mary Paul, Harry's wife, for her feedback and steadfast support for this project.

Margret McBride, our great agent, and her fantastic staff: Donna DeGutis, Faye Atchison, and Anne Bomke.

Our many friends, colleagues, and subscribers

of Ross Reck's *Weekly Reminder,* who kindly read the manuscript and made all those wonderful suggestions on how to improve it.

The extraordinary team at William Morrow—especially publisher, Lisa Gallagher, and our editor, Peter Hubbard, who helped shape this book.

CONTACT INFORMATION:

For information regarding Ross Reck's speaking availability or his consulting services, please call: (602) 391-3250 or go to: www.rossreck.com.

For information regarding Harry Paul's speaking availability, please call 760-212-8993 or e-mail at thepauls@cox.net.